Happy Birthday Nate

1990 Grandma
Grandpa & Higley

How Insects Communicate

The chemical message is clear: "Get away from me!" This toad, about to eat a bombardier beetle, is sprayed by a sudden jet of a repellent chemical called quinone and loses interest.

How Insects Communicate

Dorothy Hinshaw Patent

HOLIDAY HOUSE · *New York*

Copyright © 1975 by Dorothy Hinshaw Patent.
All rights reserved.
Printed in the United States of America.

Library of Congress Cataloging in Publication Data

Patent, Dorothy Hinshaw.
  How insects communicate.

  Bibliography: p. 123
  Includes index.
  SUMMARY: Discusses the variety of ways used by
insects to communicate. Includes butterflies, ants,
bees, termites, and many others.
    1. Insects—Behavior—Juvenile literature.
  2. Animal communication—Juvenile literature.
[1. Insects—Habits and behavior. 2. Animal
communication] I. Title.
  QL496.P37   595.7′05′9   75-6699
  ISBN 0-8234-0263-0

To Ed Lindemann,
who finds insects as fascinating as I do

Contents

How Insects Communicate

1 · Telling One Another

Insects are such familiar creatures that we often take them for granted. The fly on the window, the ant in the kitchen, the bee on the flower are everyday sights to us. They may be common, but even so insects are among the most fascinating living things. Their variety both in appearance and in life style is almost endless. There are big insects and tiny ones, beautiful insects and ugly ones, social insects and solitary ones.

One thing all insects have in common, however, is the need to communicate with others of their own kind at some time of their lives. Social insects, such as bees, termites, and ants must do so every day of their lives. They must be able to tell one another where to find food and to warn one another of danger. They must be able to recognize members of their own colony as opposed to strangers. Such a complicated way of life, in which many individuals are dependent on one another, leads to complicated systems of communicating.

Most insects, however, live alone and do not depend

on others of their own kind for food or protection. Even houseflies and gnats, which are often seen in groups, are basically solitary creatures. Other insects, such as moths and crickets, seem almost always to be alone. But even the most solitary insects must communicate at mating time, when the males and females need to find one another. Solitary insects have different ways of attracting mates, but in each case the message is clear. It says, "I am the opposite sex of your species, and ready to mate." If we think about it for a moment, we will see that this is not such a simple message. If both sexes have signals, they must be different so as not to confuse things. Each species must have its own special signals, so that time won't be wasted answering the signals of other species. And finally, only individuals which are ready to mate should give out signals or answer them.

Getting the Message Across

Each kind of living thing has its own ways of communicating with its fellows. We humans use mostly our voices. Our eyes also tell us a great deal about what a person is trying to say. In some circumstances, touch says more than words can express—the reassuring pat on the shoulder, the loving kiss.

Some insects use sight, sound, and touch for communication, too. But the most common and vital type of insect communication is quite foreign to us. Man's sense of smell is poorly developed compared with that of many other animals, and we never consciously use it to communicate. The sense of smell in insects, however, is very highly developed. Some insects can detect only a few molecules of certain chemicals in the air.

Pheromones: Insect "Words"

Chemicals play a vital role in the communication of most insects and many other animals as well. When an animal produces a chemical used as a message to another of its own kind, that chemical is called a "pheromone." Sometimes a combination of two or more

Some glands containing secretions remain inside the body; some can be popped out by muscles or by an increase of blood pressure. This caterpillar of the swallowtail butterfly Papilio machaon, *on being pinched with forceps, sticks out the pronged gland behind its head.*

DR. THOMAS EISNER

chemicals in a particular proportion make up a certain pheromone.

Most pheromones are produced by special glands on the body. There are many different locations of these glands. Some are near the mouth, others are at the tip of the abdomen. Some are on the wings. There are cases in which the pheromones seem to be produced by the whole body of the animal; no special glands which make them can be found. Some pheromones may not be manufactured in the insects' bodies at all. Scientists have recently found evidence that the caterpillar of the oak-leaf roller moth stores up certain chemicals from the oak leaves which it eats, and that the female moth uses these same chemicals to attract male moths. When an insect releases a pheromone from a gland, the whole gland may be turned inside out and the pheromone thus released from inside, or the gland may be squeezed by muscles to push out the secretion.

The study of pheromones is quite recent. Most discoveries about them have been made in the last 20 years, even though cases of chemical communication were known long before that. One reason for the delay in research into such an interesting and important field is the unfamiliar nature of the subject. People—including scientists—find it hard to think in terms of communicating by smell.

A human being's sense of smell is important mainly in connection with food. If you smell a nice, juicy steak on the charcoal broiler, you may feel hunger you didn't know you had before the steak came along. The smell of the steak has aroused a feeling in you. In other animals, a smell can arouse other feelings. The smell of a female dog in heat attracts the male and makes him feel aggressive toward other male dogs. In many social insects, the smell of certain chemicals alarms the members of the colony and warns them of danger.

The Insect "Machine"

When we discuss the reactions of insects to smells, sights, or sounds, we must keep in mind that the nervous system of insects is very different from ours. Although much insect behavior is very complicated, insects are incapable of thought. They are like small, living computers which react in set ways to the influences of the world around them. When we smell that steak, we think to ourselves "Am I ever hungry! I'd sure like to eat that." But when an insect smells the odor of a plant which serves as its food, its nervous system stimulates its muscles to move its body toward the increasingly strong odor. Once it has arrived at the leaf its mouthparts are stimulated to open and to begin biting and chewing. The insect doesn't think about what it is doing; it just does it. This makes insect behavior quite predictable. A certain stimulus given to a particular kind of insect under certain conditions

Most insects might be called a set of receiving organs ready to stimulate it into action: eyes that see, antennae that feel objects and sense odors, legs that sense vibrations in the ground, hearing organs that receive sound messages, touch-sensitive hairs and bristles, surface sensors that respond to chemical messages. This long-horned beetle has most of these—and perhaps several more, for scientists are just beginning to understand the bodies and behavior of a few kinds of insects, and there are well over 250,000 species of beetles alone.

will result in a behavior pattern that one can ordinarily be sure of.

Primers and Releasers

Pheromones which cause a predictable reaction soon after an animal becomes aware of them are called "releaser pheromones." There are many kinds of releaser pheromones. Some are produced at breeding time to attract mates. In social insects they are used to mark trails leading to food and to alarm nest mates when danger threatens the colony.

There is another kind of pheromone found in social insects and in some other animals as well, called "primer pheromones." These do not have an immediate effect on the animal receiving them; the effect is delayed. They act on the hormone systems of animals to change the functioning of the body. This finally results in a change in behavior. Sometimes the same pheromone will have both primer and releaser effects. And sometimes the pheromone may prevent certain behavior instead of cause it. An example from the complicated life of the honeybee will make this clear.

Queen Substance

The honeybee queen is a large female which lays eggs. Queens are produced in the spring from eggs laid in special queen cells. The larvae which become queens are fed special food by the workers. Honeybee workers are also females, but they do not ordinarily lay eggs. The queen produces a pheromone called "queen substance" which prevents the worker's ovaries from producing eggs. It also prevents the workers from building queen cells.

The workers receive this substance from the queen

when they groom her body, and it is distributed throughout the hive as the workers feed and groom each other. As long as there is a queen in the colony, the workers receive enough queen substance to keep them from building queen cells and to keep their ovaries from producing eggs.

When the queen dies, the workers begin to construct emergency queen cells within a few hours. Therefore the effect of the lack of queen substance on the building of queen cells is a releaser effect. The behavior of the workers is held back, or inhibited, only as long as there is queen substance in the hive. When the queen substance is gone, the workers' inhibited urge to build queen cells is "released."

It takes several days, however, for the workers' ovaries to begin to produce eggs. This is a primer effect. It takes a while for the hormone system of the workers' bodies to get egg production under way. Eventually, when the eggs are ready, egg-laying will result.

Other Means of Communication

When insects "talk" by touching, they often are combining touch with chemical communication. One insect is sensing the chemicals on the body of the other with its antennae. Scientists have found many pheromones which are apparently chemically bound to the body surface of insects and are not released into the air. Insects also use touch in their mating behavior

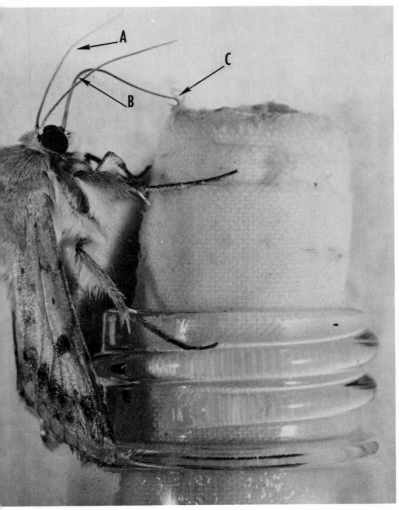

Chemical sensitivity in a corn earworm moth. While the antennae (A) receive odors from sugar water in the wick, the proboscis, a feeding tube that is very flexible (B) prepares to suck it up. Taste sensors are located at C.

7602043

as a means of coordinating their readiness to mate and as a way of assuring that they are going to mate with one of their own kind.

Many insects are silent. Others must rely completely on the sounds they make to relay their messages. Everyone is familiar with the singing of crickets and cicadas in the late summer or fall. The sounds you hear are made by the males, calling to the females. In some insects, the females also make sounds which tell the males where they are.

Taste sensors at the end of the coiled proboscis of a cabbage looper moth, as seen very highly magnified by a scanning electron microscope. The two sausage-shaped organs, called styloconicas, are found also on the antennae of moths. DR. PHILIP CALLAHAN, THELMA CARLYSLE, USDA

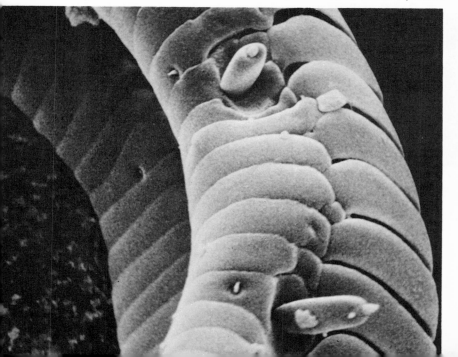

In all these cases, the sound is carried through the air, and the sound waves are picked up from the air by the receiving insect.

In other cases, however, the sound is picked up by the receiving insect through the vibrations of the surface on which it is standing. An example of this is the alarm sounds of some termites that are made when individuals bang their heads rapidly on the roof of the nest. If these sounds are recorded and played back to the animals, they do not respond to them, because they cannot hear them through the air. They do, however, have very small "hearing" organs on their legs which are especially sensitive to the vibration frequency caused by head-banging. If this seems strange to you, think of a time when you heard a sonic boom and felt the vibrations throughout your body, or when a phonograph was turned very loud and you felt the floor vibrating from the bass notes. You feel such vibrations with your whole body, while insects such as termites feel them with their special receptors.

Vision is important to communication in some insects, including butterflies and fruit flies. Glowworms and fireflies rely exclusively on visual signals to find a mate. Among social insects, however, sight is rarely used for communication. After all, the group life of social insects goes on mostly inside a dark hive or nest. The ability to see has even been lost completely in the workers and soldiers of most termite species.

Sight is much less important in insect communication than in the language of many other kinds of animals. Because of their small size, it is hard for insects to find one another by sight alone. A field of grass is much like a forest of tall trees to an insect. Besides, the small size of insects makes them ideal food for other creatures. An insect which is conspicuous enough for another insect to see is also easy for a predator to zero in on.

In some insect relatives, such as spiders and crabs, which are better equipped than most insects to take care of themselves, vision plays an important part in communication. Other invertebrate animals use other means. A few examples of these systems are described in the last chapter.

2 · Insects Sense Their Domain

It is almost impossible for a human to imagine what it's like to be an insect. A fly is not a little human with six legs and wings. To start with, the insect's body is completely different from ours. We have an internal skeleton, with bones on the inside. Insects have an external skeleton covering their bodies like armor. It is made up largely of a protein substance called chitin. The muscles of the insect are attached to this skeleton and pull against it when they contract, just as our muscles pull against our bones.

For the insect to be able to move, there must be thin, flexible joints in this skeleton. If you look closely at an enlarged picture of an ant or other insect, you can see the joints in the legs, along the body, and even in the antennae. The sense organs of the insect must also occupy thin places in the chitin, so that living nerve cells from the inside can react to what goes on outside. Some insect sense organs are large enough to see, such as the eyes, but others may be hidden away in surprising places.

This corn earworm moth, feeding on sugar water from a paint brush, shows clearly (arrow) *the opening of its hearing organ, which can hear sounds above human audibility. The moth's eye is adapted for brightness at the moment, since it is feeding in daylight; its center looks black and it has a large green edge.*

Hearing the Sounds and Sensing the Tremors

Some insects, such as many night-flying moths, have large and obvious hearing organs on their abdomens. Cicadas and some grasshoppers have similar abdominal "tympanal organs." These consist of a membrane stretched over a ring of chitin, much like the head of a drum (*tympanon* means "drum" in Greek) with an air space underneath. When sound waves cause the membrane to vibrate, the nerve endings of sense cells attached to the inner side of the membrane are moved, stimulating them to send signals to the central nervous system. Tiny tympanal organs are found on the fore-legs of some other kinds of grasshoppers and crickets.

Another type of sound receptor is found on the legs

A sound receptor ("swollen" portion at A) on the leg of a katydid, a type of grasshopper. The ear of this particular species senses airborne sound vibrations; leg receptors on many insects respond to vibrations in earth or wood. The file and scraper that produce the katydid's familiar sound are at the spot (B) where the wings begin to lie against each other. Note the useful hooked front foot.

DR. PHILIP CALLAHAN

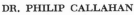

of many kinds of insects, including bees, ants, grass-hoppers, and termites. While the tympanal organs sense airborne sound, these other receptors pick up sound vibrations from the ground. They are microscopic in size, but often very sensitive to vibrations.

Seeing the Surrounding World

Insects have eyes which are very different from ours. Instead of having one lens which focuses an image onto a light-receiving surface, the insect eye has from a few to many thousand minute lenses, each of which focuses light down onto its own light-sensitive region. All the impulses from nerves attached to the separate light-sensing units of the eye are sorted out in the insect's brain. Although scientists have studied insect eyes for many years, they are still not absolutely sure exactly how they work.

Insects that use vision in their hunting or mating activities have very large eyes with thousands of individual units, allowing them to perceive a sharp image of the world around them. Insects have color vision, but it is different from ours. Insects can see ultraviolet colors which we cannot see, but many kinds, such as bees and wasps, are blind to red.

One very useful feature of an insect's vision is its ability to detect the polarized light rays. It is hard for people to understand this, since our eyes are unable to see polarization. The waves of unpolarized light com-

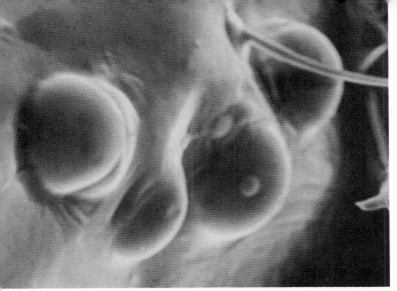

*Stemmata on the side of the head of a corn earworm cater-
pillar, highly magnified by a scanning electron microscope. These light organs of the larval stage of moths and
butterflies are sometimes incorrectly called "lateral ocelli,"
because they have some resemblance to simple adult eyes
called ocelli that are found on many insects in addition to
their compound eyes.*

ing from the sun vibrate in practically all planes at
right angles to the direction in which it is traveling.
But some waves have almost all but one plane eliminated by hitting air molecules and dust; they are
then polarized, or vibrating in only one plane of direction. To us, the blue sky looks quite even; regions near
the sun look the same as those away from it. But to an
insect, the different parts of the sky look very different,
depending on the location of the sun. The light rays
coming from different parts of the sky are polarized to

different degrees. Thus an insect can detect the position of the sun in the sky even when it is hidden from view by clouds, so long as they are light enough.

Versatile Sensory Hairs

The insect body is covered with tiny hairs. They do not function particularly to keep the body warm but rather they sense what goes on around the insect. These hairs are called "sensilla" (singular: sensillum). Most of the sensilla are sensitive to touch; if one is moved, an impulse in the nerve associated with it is sent to the central nervous system. Some of the sensilla are sensitive to sound waves and others to movements of air masses. Altogether, the sensory hairs of the insect keep it in touch with the world around it with great sensitivity.

Cerci and Antennae

Many insects, such as crickets, earwigs, and cockroaches, have two long "tails," called cerci. These are not mere decorations, but function to perceive faint air currents, some airborne sounds, and sometimes sounds carried by the ground. If the tympanal organs of a female cricket are destroyed, for example, she can still hear the mating call of the male with her cerci. If the cerci are removed, the cricket cannot hear anymore.

The most versatile and complex sense organs of the insect, however, are the antennae. If you watch an ant walking along the floor, you can see it wave its antennae constantly about, sensing the air around it. The antennae are covered with an amazing array of different sensilla. Only in recent years, with the development of the scanning electron microscope, has it been possible to study in detail the great variety of sensilla on antennae. Some are hairlike, like those on the body and legs. Others are very short and stubby. Some are twisted into a spiral shape, some are cone-shaped, and others are rounded indentations called plates.

Some of the sensilla on the antennae are touch receptors. Some sense air currents. But most are concerned with olfaction, or the sense of smell. Since smell is the most important means of communication in the majority of insects, we will spend a little time looking at theories of how insects sense and recognize the pheromones of their own kind.

Ever since pheromonal attraction was first discovered, scientists have been fascinated with the tremendous sensitivity of some detection systems. A popular animal for study has been the silkworm moth. It is readily available, and the antennae of the male moth will react to a very small concentration of bombykol, the female pheromone. Scientists have used tiny electrodes placed in the antennae to study the nerve impulses from the long, hairlike sensilla which are

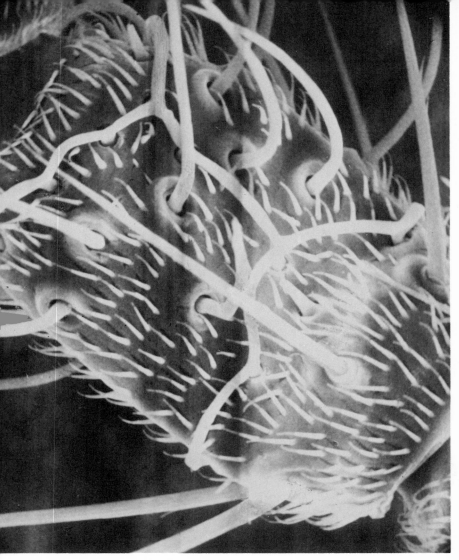

Loop sensilla on the antenna of a gall midge, a kind of fly, seen by the scanning electron microscope at a magnification of about 3000 times. Such loop shapes are found on the antennae of only certain insects.

sensitive to bombykol. They have taken pictures of the sensilla with the electron microscope to find out how they are put together.

From their studies we now know that every sensillum is supplied with one or two nerve cells which will respond to bombykol. Each sensillum is covered with one to three thousand extremely small pores which lead to a complicated system of up to 20,000 little tubules inside the sensillum. In the center of the sensillum, the ending of the nerve cell, called the dendrite (or two dendrites, if the sensillum has two nerve cells) is bathed in liquid. It is not clear yet whether the tubules reach all the way to the dendrite itself, or if they end somewhere in the liquid.

Each antenna has over 12,000 sensilla which are sensitive to bombykol. The question is, what is it about the bombykol molecule that makes the dendrites "fire;" that is, sends a nerve impulse indicating the presence of bombykol? The scientists who are doing these detailed studies of the structure and nerve impulses of silkworm moth antennae assume that the moth "smells" through what is called a stereochemical means. The stereochemical theory says that there is a match between the shape of bombykol molecules and the shape of special receptor molecules located somewhere on or in the sensillum. The two fit together like a lock and key, which causes the nerve cell to fire.

There is much evidence for this theory. Using radioactive bombykol, it has been found, for example, that the bombykol molecules become attached to the surface of the sensillum. The radiation of the molecules moves from there to the inside of the sensillum within a few minutes. These scientists believe that the bombykol molecules move through the system of pores and tubules into the sensillum and there stimulate the nerve fiber to fire. They believe that even a single bombykol molecule can cause the nerve to fire, which would explain the extreme sensitivity of the male antennae to the pheromone. Most scientists who study the insect sense of smell believe that the stereochemical theory can explain completely how insects detect various chemicals in their environment.

There are a few investigators, however, who disagree. Unfortunately, the majority of scientists appear to ignore this minority whose beliefs differ so greatly from theirs. These other scientists begin by asking why there are so many different shapes to olfactory sensilla. If they are all working by a stereochemical means, there seems to be no reason why they should have such different shapes. A hairlike sensillum should work equally well for "catching" all kinds of molecules.

This second group believes that the sensilla serve as miniature antennae, picking up the infrared radiation which is emitted by molecules, just as a television antenna picks up signals from the television station. Each kind of molecule has its own characteristic pattern of infrared radiation, and sensilla of different size and shape would best be able to pick up these different patterns of radiation. Engineers have shown that the efficiency of antennae is improved if there are small holes punched in them. This would be another way to explain the presence of pores on insect sensilla.

Perhaps these two groups of biologists will eventually be able to get together and work out a theory of insect olfaction which takes into account all aspects of the structure and function of the olfactory sensilla.

One of many kinds of sensilla found on the antennae of certain moths. According to the findings of Dr. Philip Callahan of the U. S. Department of Agriculture, sensilla act like electronic waveguides—a view for which much evidence has accumulated. These shoehorn sensilla were discovered by Callahan in 1969; they appear on a moth called the mahogany shoot borer.

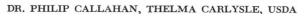

DR. PHILIP CALLAHAN, THELMA CARLYSLE, USDA

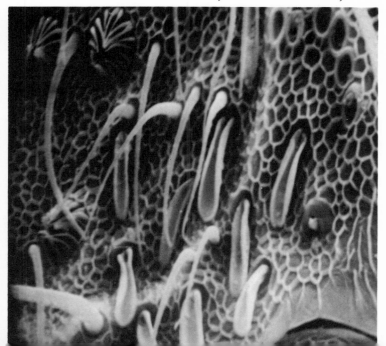

3 · The Singing Insects

Probably the form of insect communication most familiar to people is the singing of grasshoppers, cicadas, and crickets. As night falls, we enjoy the pleasant chirp of the cricket. Walking through the grassy fields in autumn, we hear the constant drone of grasshoppers singing. And in the late summer the constant whining cry of the cicada is so loud that it can annoy us. In all of these cases, the sound that we hear is the male calling to the female: Here I am, ready to mate.

Noisemakers

How do these small animals manage to produce such loud sounds? The hard external skeleton of the insect is easily modified into sound-producing areas. Most insects which produce sounds do so by rubbing one part of the body against another. If you watch a cricket sing, you will see that he vibrates his wing covers. Each wing cover has veins modified into both a

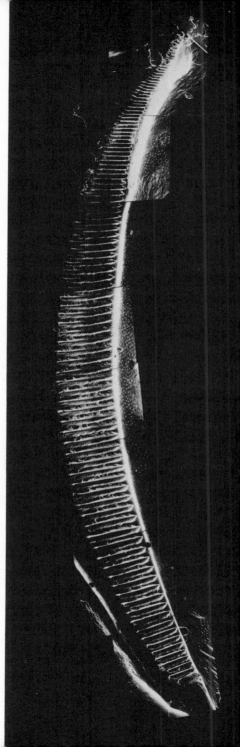

This is the toothed file on the elytron, or wing covering, of a cricket of the genus Pyrgocorapha. It was photographed in sections by an electron microscope and is reproduced at a magnification of about 200 times. The opposite elytron has a ridged edge which scrapes against this comb to produce the familiar cricket chirp.

DR. PHILIP CALLAHAN, THELMA CARLYSLE, USDA

"file" and a "scraper," and the two are rubbed rapidly together. The vibration caused by the scraping makes the wing covers vibrate as well, producing a sound that carries for quite a distance. The hind legs of grass-hoppers have a row of hard pegs or a raised ridge on the inside surface. In some kinds, the pegs are scraped along a row of ridges on the abdomen of the insect to make the sound. In others, the wing covers have a raised, hardened vein against which the leg is scraped.

Cicadas have quite a different way of producing sound. At the base of the abdomen is a drumlike organ. The "head" of the drum is a stiff membrane called the tymbal, which is supported by a hard ring made of chitin. The tymbal usually bulges outward. Attached to the tymbal is a muscle which can be contracted and relaxed very rapidly. When the cicada sings, the tymbal muscle is first contracted, then relaxed, as rapidly as 480 times a second. Each time it contracts, it pulls the tymbal inward, producing a click. When it relaxes, the tymbal snaps outward again, producing another click. Because the muscle moves so fast, the series of clicks makes what seems to be a continuous sound.

Grasshopper "Love Songs"

Sound is the best means of communication in grass-lands. Vision is very limited there for small creatures such as grasshoppers, and the grass protects these in-sects from predators which might try to find them by following their sounds. When a male grasshopper is ready to mate, he begins to sing to attract a female. The female is attracted to the call only when she is ready to mate. If she is too young, or if she has already mated, she pays no heed to his calls. But a mature female, when she hears the male, will wave her antennae about and turn toward the direction of the sound.

In some species the female gives an answering sound, and both animals move slowly toward each other. But in many, only the male can sing, and the female moves closer and closer to the sound he makes until they can see each other. As soon as the male sees the female, he changes his song and sings a "courtship song." He acts quite excited and hops about the female as he sings, and soon he jumps on her back and tries to mate. If she is not quite ready, she forces him off, and he hops about some more, singing his courtship song. This goes on until she accepts him. The male may have other songs, too, depending on the species. Sometimes he makes a special sound just before he jumps on the female, and some male grasshoppers have another song used to quiet the female if she tries to move about while mating.

Another type of grasshopper sound is called the "rivals' duet." If one male is singing to a female, and another male comes along, they face each other and sing the rivals' song back and forth. They keep on until one male gives up and leaves. However, if they become so wrapped up in their rivalry that it goes on for a long time, the female just gives up and walks away, unnoticed by her determined suitors.

Rival Cricket Males

Cricket courtship is similar to that of grasshoppers. In most kinds, only the male calls. If a female approaches him, he begins courtship singing, which may involve as many as three different songs sung in a certain order, before mating takes place. Cricket males also show rivalry, but it is more pronounced than in grasshoppers. Rival males will face each other and chirp loudly back and forth. If one doesn't leave soon, the two may fight by locking their mouth parts together and wrestling, or by kicking one another with their hind legs. The males of some kinds of crickets are so prone to fighting that the Chinese and Japanese keep them as captives and set up cricket-fighting matches, betting on which male will win much as some people bet on human boxing and wrestling matches.

The variations on grasshopper and cricket song and courtship are many. Since each species has its own song, a female can be sure of finding a male of her own kind. Females can also be attracted to the recorded sound of the males' call. Scientists have set up loudspeakers in fields and played the call of grasshoppers through them, attracting hundreds of grasshoppers this way.

Three audiospectrographs, or electronically made visible records, of calling patterns of the cricket Teleogryllus commodus. *From top to bottom, fighting signal, then the transition to courtship song, and finally the courting song itself. Each section represents slightly more than a second of time. Based on recordings by Dr. Richard D. Alexander.*

It may be, however, that in some species the call of the male has other functions. Scientists have broadcast the sounds of a kind of burrowing mole cricket through loudspeakers in a field and attracted many crickets. To their surprise, they found that more mated females were attracted than unmated ones, and 12 per cent of the attracted crickets were males. They decided that perhaps in this case the song of the male was used as a signal of a good place to set up a home rather than purely as a mating call.

Song of the Cicadas

Cicadas are not at all closely related to crickets and grasshoppers. While young grasshoppers look very much like wingless, miniature adults, the larval cicada looks very different from the adult. It spends its life underground, sucking juices from the roots of trees. Some cicadas live as long as 17 years as larvae in total darkness before emerging into the sunlight for a brief adult life.

During their few weeks as adults, the cicadas must mate and lay their eggs. Male cicadas sing from the trees. They will sing from one to four songs, then fly about a bit, then sing some more. The cicada song attracts males as well as females, and the restless flying between songs brings the males together quickly into large choruses whose singing can be heard from far away. Male cicadas do not compete like male crickets and grasshoppers. They may be so closely spaced in a tree that they bump into each other every time they fly up, but it doesn't bother them.

The females seem to be attracted to the whole congregation of males from a distance. When they reach the tree, it is not certain whether they are attracted to an individual male by sight or sound. Scientists have found it very hard to study the individual behavior of cicadas. So many individuals are so close together and so actively moving about far up in the trees that studying their behavior is quite a challenge. By marking individuals and by patiently watching, however, scientists have found that when a male and female are attracted to one another, they sit motionless on a branch facing one another, sometimes for hours on end. At other times mating takes place quickly. In either case the male does have a courtship song which is different from the calling song.

Other Songsters

Sound is important in the communication of many other insects as well. The males of some fruit flies make flutelike sounds by striking their wings against bristles

Male roaches, Periplaneta americana, *reacting to a glass rod that was dipped in an extract of the females' sex-attractant pheromone. The males have gathered about the rod and are fluttering their wings and raising the tops of their abdomens (see male at left)—behavior that is typical when they are sexually excited.*

DR. THOMAS EISNER

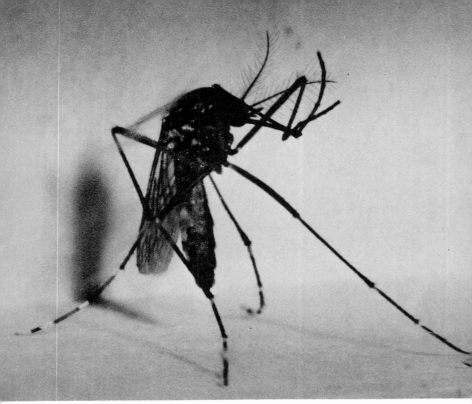

The sparsely feathery antennae of mosquitoes, seen here on a female yellow fever mosquito cleaning her proboscis, serve in mosquito communication. The male's antennae respond to a certain frequency of wing sound that means to him the presence of a female.

on their abdomens to attract females. In some water bugs, the male produces a call which makes the female swim about in circles on the water's surface. During the mating season, the male is attracted to anything which causes ripples in the water, so in this way he easily finds the female. Some cockroaches attract one another during the mating season with a combination of calls and pheromones.

Sound is very important to the mate-finding of some insects even though they have no special sound-producing organs. An interesting example of this is the yellow-fever mosquito. Males of this insect have antennae which are specially modified for sensing the sound of the wing vibrations of the female. The outer part of the antenna is slender, while the base contains an enlarged sense organ which picks up vibrations of the antenna and sends signals to the brain.

The female mosquito is larger, and her wings vibrate at a different frequency from that of the male. The antennae of the male are very sensitive to this sound. They can still hear it when the background noise is as much as 100 times as loud as the sound of the female's wings, and they are attracted from as far away as 10 inches, a considerable distance for such a small insect.

The importance of sound in the communication of most insects hasn't even been studied, although it appears to have a place in the lives of many. Part of the reason for this is that small insects may produce a wealth of sounds too soft for us to hear, so we don't even suspect that it is there. Perhaps future scientists will accept the challenge of working with such insects and will discover additional interesting uses of sound in the insect world.

4 · Molecules from Butterflies and Moths

Butterflies and moths are familiar to us all. Most butterflies are colorful creatures of the sun, found during the day sipping nectar from flowers or just flitting through the air. Most moths, on the other hand, are seen only at night. Their colors generally are dull and their size rather small, although some moths are very large and colorful. Many moths are serious pests. Some, such as the gypsy moth, attack and kill trees, while others damage food crops. The wax moths are parasites of beehives. Man has one famous, helpful moth friend. The silkworm moth has been domesticated to produce silk for so long that it can no longer fly.

Creatures of the Night

The different ways of life of butterflies and moths result in different systems of communication. Though

44

certain species of moths fly to some extent in daylight, moths as a whole are active at night. They rely mainly, therefore, on very sensitive and effective pheromone systems. The antennae of male moths are very branched and feathery, giving them a large surface area for perceiving molecules of the female's pheromones.

A very great deal of scientific research has been done on the pheromones of moths. More pheromones have been found in this than in any other group of insects. Part of the reason for this is that since so many moths are harmful to food crops or trees, they have been the subject of much laboratory work. Scientists hope that by studying the pheromones of such insects they can

An arctiid moth, Utetheisa bella, *giving off a frothy bubble of secretion from one of its neck glands; a smaller bubble can be seen coming from the second gland at the other side.* DR. THOMAS EISNER

learn how to use them for control of these pests, instead of using dangerous insecticides.

The silkworm moth is a very popular insect in pheromone research. Its system of communication is quite simple. When a female moth is ready to mate, she exposes a pair of glands at the tip of her abdomen which emit a potent pheromone. When even a minute quantity of this pheromone reaches the antennae of the male moth, he raises them and waves them about. He begins to run about in zigzags and circles, fluttering his useless wings as he goes.

If there is no wind, he keeps running aimlessly about as long as he senses the pheromone and may eventually run into the female. But if there is an air current, he turns and walks into it. He keeps pointing into the wind as long as he senses the attractant. If he loses the scent, he casts about until he finds it again and then heads into the air current once more. If there is a female upwind of him, it won't be long before he finds her. This same pattern of behavior is found in many moths, except that the males fly into the wind instead of walking. The system is so efficient that male moths have been known to find females which are a few miles away from them. A mesh cage containing a female will attract many many males in one night. Scientists hope that eventually they will be able to lure pesty moths to their death using traps baited with pheromones.

While the pheromone of the silkworm moth and others consists of one major chemical compound, scientists are discovering that the pheromones of some other moths are much more complex. For example, the female oak leaf roller moth produces a pheromone which consists of many compounds. One group of them attracts the male and another group excites him. Scientists believe that the other chemicals present in the pheromone also have effects on the males' behavior.

In many moths, the male as well as the female produces pheromones. The female angle-shades moth calls with her pheromone glands extended around dawn. The male flies to her in typical fashion, finding her exact location by touch with his antennae. He hovers close to her and just before mating, he pushes out two brushes from the tip of his abdomen. They release an odor which has an almond-like scent easily smelled by humans. Why does the male brush this scent over the female before mating? It appears that the scent from the brushes makes the female hold still; it keeps her from flying away. If the female's antennae are removed, she can no longer detect the male scent and she flies away immediately after he first touches her.

The male lesser wax moth produces a pheromone which attracts the female. But if this chemical is released into an air stream toward the female, she wanders aimlessly about flapping her wings. She cannot orient into the wind. If a male moth is placed near her, however, she can find him whether he is upwind or downwind. The male apparently produces a sound which the female uses to locate him, for if her tympanal organs are destroyed, she again wanders at random.

For many years scientists tried to mate the large and lovely oak silkworm moth in the laboratory, but their attempts always failed. Then, in 1967, the secret of why mating in the laboratory never succeeded was accidently discovered. The female of this species releases an attractant, but only when she is stimulated by a chemical from oak leaves. In this way, she never lures the male unless she is near an oak tree on which she can lay her eggs. The chances are that other insects also use such a system, and thus it is assured that food for their young is near.

Colorful Fliers

Since butterflies fly by day, it is not surprising to find that they use their eyes in finding a mate. The male butterfly does the looking, either while perching in a familiar spot or while flying about, actively hunting for a mate. In those butterflies which fly around looking, the color and pattern of a moving object must resemble that of the female to arouse the interest of the male. A male which watches from a perch, however, will fly after almost any moving object of about the right size and kind of movement, be it a fluttering leaf, a butterfly, or another insect. He must get close to

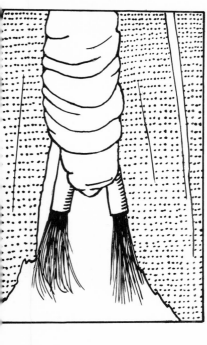

Hair pencils on a male queen butterfly pushed out about three-quarters of the way, as seen seven times actual size.

the object before he finds out if it is a female of his kind. It isn't known yet whether he recognizes her then by her behavior, her appearance, her scent, or by some combination of these methods.

So far, the mating behavior of only one kind of butterfly has been studied in detail. This is the queen butterfly, which is found in some of the southernmost United States. The queen is a relative of the familiar monarch. It has a color pattern similar to that of the monarch, but it is smaller. The male queen butterfly has scent brushes, as does the male angle-shades moth, located at the end of the abdomen. They are called hair pencils and look like tiny paint brushes. They are kept in pockets in the male's abdomen when not in use. When he pushes them out, the bunch of little hairs on the end fan out.

The male queen butterfly perches while waiting for a female. If he sees one and pursues her, he flies over her and in front of her, brushing at her antennae with his extended hair pencils. These organs are covered

DR. THOMAS EISNER

Hair pencils fully extended on a male queen butterfly.

with minute particles of sticky dust which contain the male pheromone. The particles stick to the female's antennae, and the pheromone causes her to slow down and land among the plants. The male flutters around her and continues to brush her. When she is ready to mate she folds her wings. He then pulls in his hair pencils, lands next to her, and they mate. Scientists have shown that the hair pencils are essential to successful mating. If they are removed, the male butterfly does not change his behavior, but he cannot keep the female from flying off.

The males of many butterflies, including the queen, also have glands called scent pockets on their wings. Every few seconds, when not mating, they stick their hair pencils into the scent pockets. Mating is still successful if the scent pockets are removed, however, so it isn't known yet just what their function is.

Scent brushes are found in the males of many kinds of butterflies and moths, but the pheromone is not always associated with dust particles. One hopes more species will be studied soon, and that we will know more of the variety of mating systems in these familiar but fascinating insects.

5 · Dancers of the Air

Vision may be of less importance in insect communication generally than it is in larger animals, but it is used in fascinating ways by a variety of insects large and small. For example, males of many tiny insects such as gnats and some mosquitos form large swarms in strategic places which may attract the females. In this chapter, we will see how three totally different insects use their visual senses to find mates.

Flashes in the Night

To people east of our Rocky Mountains, the end of the summer is often marked by the delightful sight of dancing fireflies. As dusk falls, first there is darkness. Then suddenly a miniature display of fireworks begins over meadows and streams. Male fireflies rise out of the grass and flit about, often dipping and diving in flight as they flash their lanterns. Each kind of firefly has a certain kind of place where it puts on its displays. While one species likes open meadows, another kind prefers the edge of the woods and another the shore of a woodland stream. Each has its own time of the evening, too, during which it displays, and the peak of activity rarely lasts more than an hour.

The flash pattern of each species is recognized by the females, which sit on grass stems during the display of the males and answer with flashes of their own. The female waits for a certain definite interval after the male flash before she answers him. He recognizes the "code" and flashes back. As he flies closer, they flash back and forth until he lands close to her. They continue flashing to each other as he walks the rest of the way, and then they mate.

With a little practice, a person with a flashlight can imitate the flash pattern of the local fireflies and make

Firefly larvae, left, have a pair of luminous organs in the case of some species and these may give off light even before hatching from the egg. Both males and females of the adult, right, have light organs that flash mating signals.

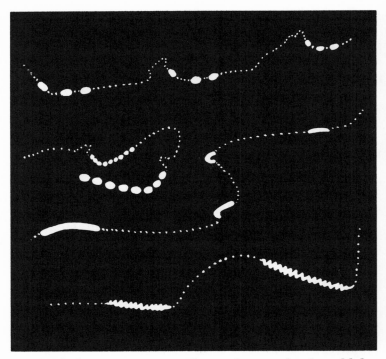

Firefly flash messages vary. These white circles, long blobs, and zigzags represent the flash patterns of different species as they would look in a time-lapse photograph; those that are enlarged represent those flashes made nearer the observation point. Dotted lines between flashes show flight paths. Based on research by Dr. James E. Lloyd.

them answer back. In this way, males can be lured to land right on the flashlight. Most species of fireflies have a simple signal; the male gives one flash of a certain length, and after the proper interval the female answers with a single flash. Some kinds, however, use a more complicated flickering flash.

The lanterns of fireflies and their relatives are located on the underside of the abdomen. In some kinds there are rows of glowing spots, while in others only one or two large lanterns are present. In most fireflies, the lanterns of the males and females are of different shapes. The females of many species cannot fly, and their bright light organ remains in one spot, attracting the dimmer male. If both sexes can fly, the males' lanterns are usually brighter. As would be expected, fireflies have especially large eyes.

Not all fireflies flash their light organs on and off to give rapid signals. The female of the European glowworm, for example, lies on the ground in the same position night after night, emitting an almost continuous glow. Sometimes she attracts hundreds of males by this simple means. The females of some other species light up only when they see the continuous glow of the male.

Some Asian fireflies produce spectacular displays when thousands of males gather in trees along a river and flash a hundred times a minute in unison, lighting up whole trees at a time. Females are found in the trees, too. The swampy ground in the areas where they are found would make ground-mating difficult, so these species use trees instead.

Sometimes successful predators tune in on the communication system of their prey and use it to their own advantage. A perfect example of this behavior is found in some female fireflies which imitate the response signal of the females of another species mating in the area, thereby luring the unwitting males into their hungry mandibles, or jaws.

"My Beautiful Balloon"

One day in 1875, an insect collector was walking through the woods in the Alps. His eye was caught by brilliant flashes of silvery light darting among the sunbeams which filtered through the trees. He swished his insect net through the air to catch one of these strange creatures and was puzzled to find only a dull, ordinary-looking little fly. Not understanding how such a plain creature could produce such a striking sight, he searched his net more carefully and found a tiny, filmy hollow bit of sparkling material caught in the net. When he tried to pick it up, his breath blew it away. Not knowing what he had found, he caught more and more of the silver flashers and always found his net containing dull male flies and little sparkling balloons.

Others were soon interested in these strange little flies and presently found that they carried the little balloons with their legs as they flew about. There were many ideas about the function of the balloons; one fanciful fellow believed that they were a kind of surfboard on which the flies cavorted among the sunbeams. Others felt that they served to warn predators to avoid the flies; the fact that the flies are not distaste-

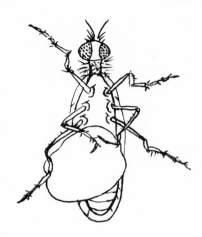

The male of the balloon fly Empimorpha geneatis *carrying its balloon. The balloons are not actually spherical, but being clutched by the legs, are flattened against the body and somewhat irregular in shape.*

ful to other insects didn't seem to bother them. Other more thoughtful persons took a clue from the fact that only males carried balloons and concluded that they were used to attract the females.

Now we know a lot more about balloon flies (also called dance flies), and the speculation that they serve to attract the females is now known to be partly correct. But there is more to the story than that. Balloon flies are predators on other insects. In predatory insects the male risks being eaten as prey by the female instead of becoming her mate. Many such insects have developed similar ways of avoiding this problem: the male simply gives the female a prey insect upon which she can feed during mating. For example, the male scorpion fly captures a prey insect before trying to attract a mate. Then he pushes out two scent glands on his abdomen which emit an attractant. When a female arrives, usually within two or three minutes, he pulls in the scent glands. After the male and female get into mating position, he gives her the prey to feed upon.

But the female balloon fly certainly can't eat the balloon. Only when other members of the balloon fly family are studied can we understand how the balloon evolved. In some such flies, the male gives no gift at all to the female. In others, the male captures prey and then hunts for a mate. He gives her the prey to eat while they mate. The males of some species dance together in a swarm, and the sight of the male with prey serves to stimulate the female into mating.

The beginning of the balloon is seen in species which use bits of sticky material to entangle the prey and keep it quiet. Probably the bits of white on the prey make it easier for the female to find the male. Other flies add more white stuff behind the prey to form a balloon. Now both the balloon and the prey serve to attract the female, and the female eats the prey after settling down to mate.

In the next stage, we find balloons with small, mangled prey attached to the front of the balloon. The prey is too small to be easily seen by the female and too small to eat. Now the balloon is the important thing, and it is but one step to the kinds of balloon flies which make a fluffy, sparkling, attractive balloon completely without any prey; and this is what the male gives the female during courtship.

Flying Dragons

The name "dragonfly" suggests a ferocious beast of the air, and the dragonfly lives up to its name. It is a strong flier and a determined hunter, capturing other insects on the wing. Damselflies are also familiar creatures, quite similar to dragonflies in appearance, only smaller. Both rely on their vision in their hunting and have huge eyes, so it is no surprise to find that their eyes are equally important in their reproductive life.

In many dragonflies and damselflies, the males and females have very different coloration, and the males use these differences to tell the sexes apart. How does a scientist go about determining the method of communication of such insects? Let us use the example of an American dragonfly which was recently studied. The males of this dragonfly are light blue and green, turning to a darker blue with age. The females, on the other hand, are bright yellow-green with brown stripes on their abdomen. Both sexes have clear wings. These striking differences in color suggest that color is important in sexual recognition, but proving it is something else.

The first thing the scientist did was to watch the behavior of the dragonflies without interfering. He saw that each male had his own special "roost" where he rested. Whenever another male flew near, he flew

up and attacked it. There was an area around each perch which was defended against other males by the resident. Such areas are common in the lives of many animals, such as birds, and are called "territories." If a female dragonfly flew into a male's territory, he treated her very differently from the males. Instead of attacking her, he landed on her back. If she accepted him, they would mate.

Now it was time for experiments to prove that the males used the color pattern of the females to tell them from the males. The scientist caught some dragonflies and put them into the refrigerator to slow down their movement. He painted some of the males to look like females and painted some of the females to look like males. He then tied a harness of light cotton thread around the thorax of the dragonfly he was ready to try out first. He tied the other end of the thread to a five-foot-long fishing pole. When the dragonfly warmed up it could fly, but the scientist could control its movements and watch closely to see how it was treated by the free male dragonflies. He also used dead dragon-

The compound eyes of various flies, beetles, and other insects are complicated structures containing many individual light-gathering organs. Each individual organ has a small lens (at left in this picture) behind which is a crystalline cone, a pigment cell and filament and finally a light-sensitive cell connected by a nerve fiber to the brain.

DR. PHILIP CALLAHAN

flies in the same way. He found that free males treated normal females, dead females, and males painted like females all as if they were normal females, whereas normal males, dead males, and females painted as males were all treated as males. This proved that only vision was involved in the discrimination of males from females. If scent had been a factor, painted males would be treated differently from normal females.

When he painted the wings of some females black, the scientist had a very interesting result. The males of the species he was using ignored these females, but males of another kind which has black on its wings tried to court them.

Some dragonflies and damselflies have more elaborate mating behavior. For example, let's take a damselfly with colored wings. The males have bright ruby-red wing bases, while the females have amber wing bases. The males of this species have definite territories and attack any males which enter them. But instead of sitting on their perches waiting for females to pass by, they try to attract females by flying up about a foot into the air every half minute or so, rapidly beating their wings and showing their bright red color. If a female ready for mating enters the territory, she hovers in one place until the male comes to her. If he should approach a female which isn't ready to mate, she will spread her wings and bend her abdomen. The male gets the message, gives up and returns to his perch.

6 · *Tree-Destroyers:*
The Bark Beetles

All the insects you have met so far in this book have very little to do with one another except at mating time. They have no need to cooperate with each other in any other way, so their communication systems are relatively simple. In this chapter we will see how several different chemical signals can combine with one another and sometimes also with sound to coordinate the activities of insects at a crucial time of their lives.

Introducing the Bark Beetles

There are many kinds of bark beetles, but we are going to look at only the ones which often kill trees to make homes for themselves. You might think that a creature capable of killing a tree would have to be quite large, but bark beetles are less than a quarter of an inch long. They are serious forest pests in many

63

parts of the country, and many scientists have devoted years to studying their way of life. If their means of communication can be understood, it can perhaps be used against them to keep them from killing trees.

How do such small creatures kill big trees? They do it by working together, thousands of beetles boring into the bark of the tree at the same time until the tree cannot survive the damage. Some bark beetles carry a fungus with them which also attacks the tree as they bore in, weakening it further. If the tree is not killed, the beetles cannot live there, for the pitch the tree produces as a defense mechanism will clog their tunnels and, in some cases, will poison the beetles. Thus it is very important that many beetles be attracted to the same tree at the same time so that they can overwhelm the tree's defenses.

Southern Pine Beetles

In many species of bark beetles, the females fly in search of a suitable tree. Some beetles are restricted to one kind of tree, while others can successfully attack several different kinds. In either case, the first females are apparently attracted by the smell and sight of the tree.

The southern pine beetle has been studied in detail. Upon landing, a female will walk around exploring the bark. No one knows for sure yet just how the female decides to attack a certain tree, but when she does she bores into a crevice in the bark. At the same time, she releases a very potent pheromone. The combination of the pheromone and the resins released from the tree as she bores acts to attract large numbers of beetles very rapidly. At this stage more males than females are attracted. After landing, however, the males release a different pheromone which inhibits the attraction of other males. In this way, a balance of male and female beetles is reached.

Meanwhile, all the beetles are boring away at the tree, and it is resisting by pouring out resin. As long as it can produce resin, it is not possible for the beetles to feed. The females keep sending out the pheromone that interacts with the resins, attracting more beetles. As more arrive, the concentration of the male phero-mone keeps increasing until it begins to inhibit both

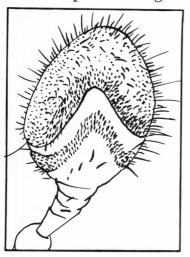

The tip of the flagellum, or sensory part, of the antenna of an ips bark beetle. The spines are sensilla that detect the odors of other bark beetles' pheromones and the odors of tree resins.

males and females from landing, so they fly to nearby trees and begin to attack those.

When the tree's resistance is finally broken, it stops producing resin. The beetles can now eat. When the female feeds, the production of her pheromone is inhibited. Now there is no more resin and no more pheromone, so new beetles no longer come to that tree. Enough were attracted to kill the tree and no more.

Other Bark Beetles

The communication systems of other bark beetles are similar to that of the southern pine beetle, but there are several variations. Both the male and the female of the western pine beetle produce attracting pheromones, for instance. Predators on these beetles are also brought to the invaded tree by this odor. Thus the predators are tuning in on the beetles' communication system to find their prey.

Very recently scientists have found that some bark beetles also use sound in their communication systems. The Douglas-fir beetle is apparently first attracted solely by the resins of the tree. At this stage, two females arrive for every male. Then the females release an attracting pheromone, and more beetles arrive, but this time there are two males to every female. The attraction ends suddenly. While investigating the reason for the abrupt end of attraction, scientists found that the male can rub his wings over his body and make a

A bark-beetle egg gallery. Note the even spacing, indicating that the females are able to avoid each other as they bore.

sound which the female can hear from inside the wood. When she hears it, she apparently produces a second chemical which covers up the attracting effect of the first pheromone. In this way, once an individual female has a mate for herself, she attracts no more beetles.

Sound may play still another part in bark beetle communication. The females of some species make soft clicking noises while they are inside the bark. If other females are nearby, the rate of clicking increases greatly. Since the holes bored by females are remarkable evenly spaced on the tree, it is possible that these clicking noises identify places in the bark which are already occupied, so that newly arrived females will avoid them.

Male Pheromones

In other kinds of bark beetles, the males make the first attack. They bore into the wood and make a hollow space where their two or three mates can gather. But they do not release a pheromone right away. They

must bore and eat first, so that by the time the pheromone is produced, there is a "home" for the attracted
females. When a female lands near the entrance hole
of a male's tunnel, she makes a sound by rubbing a
special part of her head against the inside of the hard
armor covering her body. Then she enters the tunnel.
If the sound-producing structures are removed, she
cannot make the sound and is attacked by the male
when she tries to enter.

Because of the destructive behavior of the bark
beetles, many scientists are working hard to unlock
the secrets of their coordinated attacks on trees and
logs. As more is learned about them, the communication systems of these beetles will probably turn out
to be even more complicated than they now appear.

7 · Social Insects: The Amazing Ants

The human race has always been fascinated by the social insects, perhaps because their cooperative way of life is at once so similar to and so different from its own. As we learn about how their societies are held together, we will see that the similarities are really few and the differences overwhelming.

A tendency toward social life is found in many kinds of insects. There are beetles, bugs, and crickets which care for their young, and caterpillars which spin communal tents and divide up the labor. But true social behavior is found in only two orders of insects, the Hymenoptera (bees, wasps, and ants) and the Isoptera (termites). There are also many Hymenoptera which are completely solitary, and others which merely approach the true social way of living. During evolution, different groups of hymenopterans have each developed into social behavior by themselves. It is interesting to compare these systems and see how they resemble each other and how they differ.

But how do we draw the line between the earlier form that is called "presocial behavior" and true social behavior? Scientists generally agree that three conditions must be met for a species to be considered truly social. In the first place, there must be cooperation in the care and feeding of the young. Second, some of the individuals in the colony must be specialized for reproducing while others busy themselves with the work. Last, there must be some overlap of generations, so that the young which have been raised stay around and help out their older relations with the work of the colony. All ants and termites meet these standards, and many bees and wasps as well can be classified as truly social.

In spite of the independent development of social

Since biblical times the ant has been the object of close study by human beings because of its complicated social life. This species is Pogonomyrmex badius.

DR. THOMAS EISNER, DR. DANIEL ANESHANSLEY

behavior in different insects, there are certain things they all have in common. There is at least one queen, which does little or no work after the colony has been founded. There are workers, which are usually sterile and cannot reproduce. In Hymenoptera all workers are females, and males are produced only during the swarming season. Termites, on the other hand, have both kings and queens which live in the colony at all seasons. Termite workers are of both sexes as well.

The work of the colony is divided up among the workers, often by age. The younger workers tend to take care of the brood (eggs and recently hatched young) while older workers go out and collect food. Many termite and ant species also have soldiers, which are individuals with especially well developed jaws and aggressive natures. They are very active in defense of the colony.

The variety of social life is very great. A colony of some species consists of perhaps a few dozen adults. In the fall, new queens and males fly off to mate, and only the young queens live through the winter asleep. In the spring they set up new colonies. Other species of social insects have huge perennial colonies which may last for years and years. All stages between these extremes are found. The largest colonies of social insects are those of a kind of the African driver ant, which can consist of as many as 22 million workers. The total weight of all the ants in such a colony would be about ten pounds.

Mutual Attraction

The most basic form of communication necessary to the existence of social insects is an attraction among the individuals in the colony. If some termites or ants are captured and released into a bare container in the laboratory, they will soon cluster together in little groups. If a queen is present, many of the workers will gather around her, and if larvae are present, they also become the focus of worker attention. Scientists believe that the basis of this attraction is in "surface pheromones," substances perhaps chemically attached to the exoskeleton of the insects or at least closely associated with it. Experiments have shown that there is indeed attraction between individuals, although sometimes other factors are involved. For example, fire ant workers move to areas where there is more carbon dioxide—which means places where there are more ants, since carbon dioxide is produced during respiration.

While workers are attracted to one another, the queen has the greatest drawing power, with the larvae second. The queen of a colony is constantly surrounded by workers which lick her and feed her. She may be completely hidden from view by the huge swarm of workers attending to her needs. If the chemicals from the body of the queen are extracted and applied to the surface of a dummy, the workers will treat the dummy as if it were a live queen.

The attractiveness of the brood is also probably based on surface pheromones. Scientists have extracted chemicals from the larvae of the fire ant and then coated corn-cob grits, clay particles, and bits of paper with the extracts. These bits of nonliving matter were then treated just like larvae by the workers. For hours they were groomed and rubbed, and when the colony was disturbed, the workers ran around carrying the grits, just as if they were larvae which needed to be saved from an enemy.

In addition to the attraction among individuals, there is also apparently a "colony odor" peculiar to each colony. Scientists believe the colony odor derives mainly from the kind of foods used by the colony at any given time. If an ant or bee mistakenly tries to enter the wrong nest, it will almost certainly be attacked because of its different odor.

The Variety of Ant Life

Ants are by far the most varied of the social insects, with many fascinating variations of community life found among them. They are also the most widely distributed social insects, and are found from the arctic tree line to the southern tips of South America and Africa, on Tasmania, and on most oceanic islands. Ants outnumber other social insects, both in total number of individuals and in number of species. As a matter of fact, there are more different species of ants than of all other social insects combined.

Among the ants in a colony that lead specialized lives, those chosen to be "honeypots" certainly have a strange function. These ants of the genus Myrmecocystus are distended with honey stored in their abdomens, which serves as a reserve food for the colony in dry or inhospitable places. The ants wanting food tap them and the honeypots regurgitate some honey, as automatically as a slot machine. The bar across the top of each abdomen is one of the ant's sclerites, protective plates that were originally close across the abdomen; the greater part of the "pot" is a stretchable membrane that connects the sclerites.

Many ants are highly specialized in their way of life. Some are found only living inside of certain kinds of plants. Others have feeding specialties; some eat nothing but fungus which they grow in special "gardens" inside their nests. Others eat only the eggs of other insects, and some eat only other kinds of ants.

As with many kinds of living things, the greatest variety of ants is found in the tropics. Ants are very important there, since they are the greatest tropical predators of invertebrate animals. The social organization of ant colonies varies as well, with some kinds having only one queen and others more than one. Some ant species lack soldiers, and others have soldiers as well as two sizes of workers. Some ants live in large, elaborate, permanent nests under the ground while others, such as army ants, never dig a nest, but always make camp on the surface. Because of the great variety of ant life, it is difficult to speak of how "ants" communicate. So keep in mind that the examples here are only that and do not necessarily represent conditions in the life of all ant species.

Alarm and Defense

If an ant colony is to survive, it must be able to warn its members of danger and defend itself against enemies. These two functions are inseparably bound together in the life of an ant colony, for in many species the same chemical that warns of danger also repels the invaders.

DR. THOMAS EISNER

In colonial life there is constant cooperation in many ways, so communication among ants, bees, termites, and other social insects is highly important. One ant here is giving food to the other; their mouthparts are in contact and the liquid food is passed from the crop of one to the other. The species is Camponotus herculaneus.

The communication of alarm has apparently evolved separately several times in ants as a whole, for various species show four different types of glands producing alarm substances. There are certain general characteristics of these substances. First, the alarm signal must fade rapidly if it is not reinforced. If a worker encounters an enemy invading the nest, for example, it releases the alarm substance. When the molecules of the pheromone reach other nearby workers or soldiers, they join in the defense, and if they cannot handle the situation alone, they also release alarm substance. When enough defenders have arrived to deal with the intruder, the signal must die out fast, or too much of the nest will be disturbed.

Second, the reaction of the ants to their alarm substances varies with the nature of the colony. In species with small colonies which live close to the surface of the soil or in rotting logs, the most likely alarm reaction is panic. A small concentration of alarm pheromone will cause workers to run wildly about. A few workers will act defensively, and others will retrieve the brood and carry it off, but most of the individuals will simply scatter.

However, if the ants are a kind which have a large, permanent underground nest, such as those which raise fungus gardens, their reaction is quite different. Instead of reacting with instant panic, they are attracted to the site of the disturbance and react aggressively, trying to fight off the invaders by attacking alien objects. The workers are strongly attracted instead of repelled by their alarm pheromones. This is called aggressive alarm. Such species have more to lose by abandoning their nests, and it is worth the risk of losing many of their members to defend their home.

Stages in between pure panic alarm and aggressive alarm are found, of course. The reaction of the harvester ant depends on the concentration of the pheromone. At low concentrations it attracts the ants, but at higher concentration it puts them into an aggressive frenzy. The fire ant releases both an alarm and a trail pheromone when disturbed. The trail pheromone attracts other fire ants, while the alarm pheromone excites them.

Food-Gathering

When a worker ant finds food, there is often more available than it can bring back to the nest alone. Ants have different ways of guiding nest mates to new food finds. Species with small colonies often use a method called "tandem running," whereas those with large colonies lay pheromone trails from the food source back to the nest.

After returning to the nest from a new food find, workers of some ants which use tandem running make a special display called "invitation behavior" to attract another worker. As the two ants run toward the food, the follower keeps touching the leader with its antennae. The follower is keeping track of the leader partly by sensing a pheromone released onto the body of the leader.

Other ants have a more complicated system called "tandem calling." When the successful scout ant returns to the nest, it raises its abdomen and pushes out the sting. A drop of an attracting pheromone clings to the sting. When the first ant attracted by this pheromone reaches the calling ant and touches it, the pair runs off toward the food source. The follower keeps touching the leader's abdomen and hind legs with its antennae. The attracting pheromone keeps stimulating the follower. If somehow the two insects lose contact, the leader stops and raises its abdomen again, "calling"

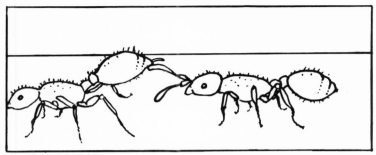

An ant of the species Leptothorax acervorum *has pushed out its odorous sting at the tip of its abdomen. A nest mate arrives, attracted by the odor, and keeps touching the abdomen and legs of the leading ant as they hurry off to newly found food.*

until the follower touches its body. Then they continue on their way.

Tandem running and tandem calling bring only one extra worker to a food source at a time. This works fine for small colonies, but it takes a lot of food to feed a large ant colony. Thus some means must be present to communicate the presence of food so that the right number of workers can go to collect from each food find. For this purpose, ants use trail substances. Ant workers are constantly going out to explore and hunt for food.

If a worker finds a choice piece, such as the body of a dead insect, it inspects it thoroughly, then returns to the nest. On the return trip, the worker drags the tip of its abdomen over the ground, laying a chemical trail as it goes. Like alarm substances, trail pheromones appear to have evolved separately many times among the ants, since five different glands are involved in different species.

In any case, when other workers encounter the trail, they immediately follow it to the end and gather some food, laying their own trail on top of the original one on the way home. If a worker finds no food at the end of the trail, or if there are already so many ants swarming about the food so it cannot get to it, it does not lay a trail on its way back to the nest. Since the attraction of the trail depends on its strength, this method allows the right number of ants and no more to go to any one food source. The trails of most ants do not last long, so when the food source is exhausted, the trail soon fades and the ants do not waste time going to worn-out sources.

The trail-laying behavior of fire ants has been studied in great detail. A worker can detect a fresh trail from almost a half inch away, and follows it right away. Fire ants act as just described for ants in general, except that often their trails are long-lasting. They may build roofs over old trails or make galleries in the soil leading out from the nest. In this way they are protected on their way out of the nest, and their food-gathering area is increased.

Fire ants also use trail-laying pheromones during their frequent moves. If a worker finds a good nest site, it lays a trail back to the old nest. Other workers follow the trail and inspect the site. If they think it is a good one, they also lay a trail home. When a strong enough trail is laid, the whole colony moves along it to the new spot.

Other kinds of ants lay exploratory trails. When army ants are staying in one place, their workers lay trails continuously as they go out from the colony. These exploratory trails may last for days or weeks and be used over and over again.

The Slavemakers

One of the most interesting developments in ant evolution is that of the slavemaker ants. These species raid the nests of other ants and make off with the pupae. When the adults of the slave species emerge from the pupae, they accept the slavemakers as nest mates and work as hard for them as they would for their own kind. Some slavemakers have become so completely specialized as raiders that they are totally dependent on the slaves for their everyday needs.

Some slavemakers owe their success to their ability to use the communication system of the slave species to their own advantage. These slavemakers species have very enlarged glands, which produce huge quantities of pheromones. These substances act as aggressive alarm substances to the slavemakers and as panic alarm substances to the slaves. When they raid a slave-species nest, the slavemakers spray any defending ants with these chemicals. While attracting and exciting more of the slavemakers, the pheromones panic the slaves and make them scatter, leaving their brood an easy mark to the invaders.

Social Parasites

Ants are not the only creatures which have learned to use the communication systems of other ants. Many different kinds of beetles, mites, and other small animals live in ant colonies right along with the ants, sharing the protection of their nest and often their food. Some of these are barely tolerated by their hosts, while others have mastered the communication system of their victims so well that they receive better treatment from the ants than they give one another.

A fascinating example of the most successful social parasite is a European beetle which lives with a kind of wood ant. The beetle lays its eggs among the brood of the ant, and the beetle larvae are totally accepted by the worker ants. This is because a beetle larva produces an attractant from its skin which probably duplicates the attractive pheromone of the ant larvae. When it wants to be fed, it imitates the begging behavior of the ant larvae; it taps the lip of the adult ant worker, which makes the ant regurgitate a drop of food. The beetle larvae are much more intense in their begging than are the ant larvae, so they get the lion's share of the food. Not only that, but in their spare time they also eat the ant larvae, so they have plenty of food. Fortunately for the ants, the beetle larvae also eat one another, so only a few remain in any one ant colony.

After the beetle leaves its pupa, it departs from the wood ant colony in search of the home of a different kind of ant, one that eats insects. The wood ants do not raise a brood in the winter, while the insect-eating ants do. Thus, by leaving the wood ant colony, the beetle assures itself of a food supply through the winter. Before leaving, the beetle tanks up by inducing the workers to feed it. It begs for food by drumming on a worker with its antennae, then touching its mouthparts to make it give up a drop of food. This mimics perfectly the behavior of the ants themselves when they beg food from each other.

The beetle finds the new ant colony by its scent. When it gets there, the beetle waits outside the entrance. It taps on a passing ant with its antennae and then raises the tip of its abdomen toward the ant. The ant licks a special secretion from the beetle's abdomen, which keeps it from attacking the beetle. Then the ant is attracted to glands along the sides of the beetle's abdomen. These glands produce a chemical which fools the ant into accepting the beetle as one of its own. Thus they are called "adoption glands." Probably the adoption glands secrete a substance identical to or similar to the odor of the ant species itself. In any case, after smelling the adoption secretion, the ant picks up the beetle and carries it right into the nest. There it is accepted and fed just as if it were an ant, but it gets away with doing no work. In the spring, the beetle again leaves and finds a wood ant colony in which to lay its eggs, beginning the cycle anew.

8 · The "Talk" of Honeybees

Honeybees have been praised for their hard work and for their delicious honey since the days of the ancients. They have been studied by curious scientists for centuries. But it is only in this century that the varied means of communication which make a honeybee colony work smoothly have been discovered. You have already learned how the queen substance affects the life of the hive. In this chapter we will concentrate on the unique means of communication used by honeybees to let one another know where to find the best sources of food. This is especially important now since one of the scientists to share the 1974 Nobel Prize was the German Karl von Frisch. Since the early part of the century he has studied the life of the honeybee and has made fascinating discoveries about honeybee communication.

The organization of the honeybee hive is simpler than that of some ants and termites. There is one queen bee and from 20,000 to 80,000 workers, all females.

Every year, in the spring, male bees called drones are produced, and new queens. The raising of the queens is made possible by an annual drop in the level of queen substance each spring. The old queen leaves the hive with a swarm of workers, and one of the new queens takes over after leaving the hive to mate with drones from other colonies. Here another effect of the queen substance is found: it attracts the drones to the young queens for mating.

Honeybees also have an alarm pheromone. When one bee stings an enemy, she releases this pheromone at the same time. It attracts other bees and excites them to attack as well. People have often discovered this the hard way, when they are stung several times more after one bee attacks them.

The workers divide up the chores of the hive, partly on the basis of age. The younger workers feed the larvae and build new combs for honey and for raising young. Older workers leave the hive to gather nectar and pollen to feed the colony. The hive is usually located in a hollow tree or in a hive built for the bees by a beekeeper. There are usually several combs which hang vertically within the hive. Some areas of the comb are used for raising young and others for honey storage.

The Round Dance

The workers which gather food are called foragers. They leave the hive and hunt around for good sources

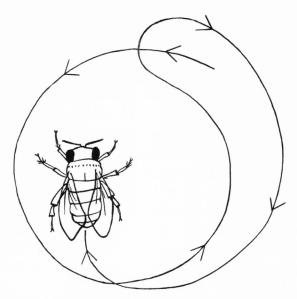

The round dance, by which a honeybee can transmit infor-mation about a nearby food location to the bees that follow it in the dance.

of food. When one has found abundant food near the hive, she collects all she can carry and returns home, transporting the nectar in her honey stomach. When she reaches the hive, she gives the nectar to other workers.

After a few successful trips to the same source, the forager begins to dance around on one of the combs, making small circles as she turns first to the right, then to the left. Other workers become very excited by this little "round dance" and crowd about her, touching her body with their antennae. One by one they leave the hive and fly out to search in the area nearby for the food source. The workers which followed the dancer about learned one thing from this round dance: Go out and get the food near the hive. They can also smell the aroma of the food source on the body of the dancer, so they know what scent to search for.

When food is close to the hive, this method works very well. One forager comes back with the message of a good place for nectar. Other bees go out and find it, too, and dance when they return, which makes still more bees go out. When the food is used up, the foragers stop dancing and stop collecting at that spot themselves; thus the efforts of the bees are not wasted.

The Waggle Dance

Often bees fly quite a distance, even for a few miles, before finding food. If a forager returned from such a distance and did a round dance, other workers would be searching all over the place looking for food. But if the food is farther away, the returning forager does a different kind of dance. It is done in a figure eight, with a straight run followed by a loop to either side. During the straight run, the dancer wags her abdomen back and forth, so the dance is called the "waggle dance." While she dances, the other bees follow her around, touching her body with their antennae, just as in the round dance.

After following one or more bees doing the waggle dance, a new forager will fly out of the hive right in the direction of the food source. Not only that, but she will fly straight and swiftly until she is near the right place before she begins to search. How did she know which way to fly and how far to fly? It is thanks to Karl von Frisch that we know the answers to these questions. It is also interesting to learn how he discovered the true meaning of the waggle dance, for it tells us something about the pitfalls of scientific research.

Early in his career, Dr. Von Frisch studied many aspects of bee behavior. He discovered the round dance and the waggle dance. However, he thought the waggle dance was used when the forager had found a good source of pollen. This is because he always set out his experimental dishes of sugar water or flowers with nectar close to the hive for convenience. Thus bees reporting nectar always did a round dance. Bees with pollen were always returning from natural sources of food more distant from the hive; thus they always did waggle dances. It wasn't until 1944, when he placed one dish of sugar water close to the hive and another one far from the hive that he accidently discovered the true meaning of the waggle dance. He was amazed to see that bees returning from the near dish did a round dance and that bees from the distant dish did a waggle dance. He also noted that bees aroused by the waggle dance flew out in the correct direction and began searching near the dish. So he set out to find out how the waggle dance showed the bees where to go.

By setting out dishes in different directions and at different distances and carefully observing the dances done by the bees, Dr. Von Frisch was able to decode the waggle dance. He decided that the distance to a food source is indicated by the length of the wagging run. The farther away the food, the longer the wagging portion of the dance. During the straight run, the bee also emits a buzzing sound. Either the duration of the sound or the time of the run shows the other bees how far to go. But the absolute distance is not given. Rather, the dancer shows the amount of energy she used to reach the food source. If she flew against the wind reaching the food, for example, the time of the run would be longer.

The means of indicating direction is even more amazing at first glance. We saw in Chapter 2 that an insect's eyes can detect polarized light from the sky. As long as a bee can see blue sky, she knows where the sun is. A foraging bee flies out to a food source at a certain angle to the sun, depending on the direction of the food and the time of day. On a hot day, she may do her waggle dance on the landing platform of the hive. If so, she directs the straight run of the waggle dance at the same angle to the right or left of the sun as she flew, effectively pointing toward the food source. But what does she do in the more usual case, when she is dancing on the vertical surface of the comb, inside the dark hive? She dances as if straight up were the direction of the sun, and points her run at the same

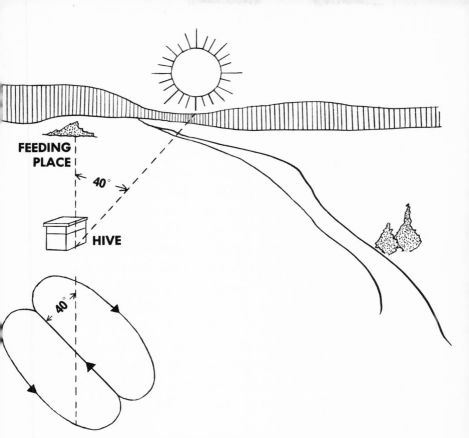

The waggle dance. The feeding place is 40 degrees to the left of the sun's position. In the waggle dance, shown here at bottom left, the forager bee points her run at the same angle away from straight up.

angle to the right or left of "up" as the angle was to the right or left of the sun when she flew out of the hive.

For example, if the forager flew straight in the direction of the sun when she left the hive, she would point her run straight up the comb. If she flew 90° to the right of the sun as she left the hive, then she would dance 90° to the right on the comb. If she flew directly away from the sun, her straight run would point straight downward on the comb, and so forth. The dancer also seems to give some information as to the abundance or sugar concentration of the food by the liveliness and enthusiasm of her dancing.

In recent years, a few other scientists have criticized Von Frisch's work, saying that his experiments never proved that the dance information was actually used by the other foragers. They said that the bees were simply excited by the waggle dance in the same way as by the round dance, to search about for flowers with a certain scent. Their criticism has led to new experiments and to re-examination of Von Frisch's old experiments, which is a good thing. But after a review of all the evidence, it becomes clear that Von Frisch and others have come as close to "proving" their case as possible.

The critics pointed out that if the bees are provided with two food sources with the same scent in two different directions, waggle dances will cause foragers to go to both places. But Von Frisch had explained this long ago. He gave the bees two sources, until there were bees going to both of them. He marked the bees going to each place with dots of different colored paint. Then he took away the food for a while. Both groups of bees stopped foraging. Every once in a while, one of the bees would fly out to her old collecting place to see if there was more food. Then he provided food at only one of the feeding tables. After finding food there once more, a forager returned to the hive and danced. Bees from both groups of foragers were excited to return to their old feeding places, so that both sites were visited. But only the site which now had food was visited by new recruits which hadn't collected at either site before. Thus the old foragers were excited to fly out to their old collecting places by the scent of the source on the body of the returning forager. They paid no attention to the information in the dance. But new foragers did heed the distance and direction information and head for the correct feeding place.

Another factor which aids the bees in finding the food source is the smells left there by previous foragers. Each bee colony appears to have a unique odor shared by all its members and probably derived mostly from the food they have been collecting. Any time a bee collects pollen or nectar from a certain flower, it leaves some of the colony odor behind when it leaves. Bees are attracted to the odor of their own colony and repelled by the odor of bees from other colonies. Also, worker bees have a special gland which produces an attracting pheromone. Often, when they land at a food source, they push out their stings and release a bit of this chemical into the air. This can attract other bees to the site, too.

The critics of Von Frisch think that these two scents, plus the sight of bees collecting at a food source, are more important in drawing bees to the right place than the waggle dance information is. They did one experiment which seemed to show that they were right on this point. They trained bees to fly to a food source a certain distance from the hive. Then they added dishes between the hive and that source to see if the new recruit bees would ignore them and fly the correct distance before landing. In their experiments, many new recruits did land at the closer dishes, as if they had not used the distance information from the dance. But as Von Frisch pointed out later, the experiment was done on a very windy day. When the wind is strong bees fly closer to the ground, and odor becomes much more important than the dance information.

It seems that the critics of Von Frisch do not realize one very important fact. Dr. Von Frisch never said that the information in the dance is the only thing which guides bees to food sources. He just says that the information is there and is used under certain circumstances. The previous experience of a forager bee is also important, as are the odors on the body of the forager, the colony odor at the site, and any pheromone released there by the forager. But the dances are important, too, and amazing as it may seem, the bees can interpret and use that information to find food.

There are several experiments which show very persuasively that bees do use the dance information, but only two of the most striking will be described here.

One experiment uses the fact that different honeybee "dialects" exist to show that the distance information is used. The honeybee is found in many different parts of the world, and different varieties of bees use slightly different dances. For example, the dark carnolian race of bees which Von Frisch used for most of his experiments changes from the round to the waggle dance for food sources about 80 yards from the hive. The yellow Italian strain, however, does a round dance to indicate distances of up to about ten yards. Then it changes to a "sickle dance," a sort of flattened figure-eight shape in which the opening of the sickle points toward the food. At about 120 yards, the waggle dance is used. The straight-run portion of the Italian bee dance is also slower for a given distance than is that of the carnolian bee.

Scientists made mixed colonies of the two types of bees. They were perfectly able to live and work together. But when it came to being able to understand the dances, trouble started. The carnolian bees which were excited by Italian dances would search too far away for the food, while Italian bees which followed carnolian dances looked too close. This seems to be pretty solid proof that the bees do use the distance information provided by the dances.

In 1970, three scientists did very elaborate experiments where they controlled for all factors—that is, eliminated them—other than the dances that they could think of which might give bees clues to the location of the food. They located the hive out in the middle of flat land with the same kind of plants all around. They even constructed a road to cross the existing one so that north, south, east, and west all looked the same. They labeled hundreds of bees with individual numbers so they could be identified. They sealed the scent glands of the bees shut. They captured the bees gently with plastic bags so that no alarm pheromones were released which might attract other bees. They rotated feeding dishes from one site to another and placed plastic on the feeding tables, which they changed every five minutes. In this way, they eliminated the factor of colony odors. They also rotated observers every five minutes, observed and described all dances in the hive, and recorded the numbers of all bees attending the dances.

They found that if a new recruit appeared at a feeding site within a few minutes of attending a dance, she went to the correct site in almost all cases. In another experiment, they provided food at dishes in opposite directions and had bees feeding at each. In this way, both dishes had bees there, in case the sight of other bees was a very important factor to a recruit in choosing where to go. But the sugar solution at one dish was too weak to inspire dancing in the foragers, while the solution at the other site was strong enough to make foragers there dance vigorously. Under these conditions, 282 out of 295 new recruits arrived at the dish with the strong solution, just as the dances "told" them to. This evidence clearly shows that the direction

Sound may be a clue to other bees when a forager does its dances in a dark hive, but scientists are not sure. The familiar hum of the honeybee is produced by its wings, which beat 190 times a second. Some scientists think many animals emit a little invisible ultraviolet radiation, which bees can see, though others don't agree about such emissions. So the idea of "seeing in the dark" to tell what the dances show is also an uncertainty.

information in the dances is perceived and used by the new recruits.

Even with all the experiments done on the dancing bees, it is a bit embarrassing to scientists that they cannot say for sure just which sense or senses the bees use to understand the dance. Sight cannot be involved, since the inside of the hive is dark. It is not known for certain whether the followers use the sound made by the dancer or the time she takes in her run to gather the distance information. Most scientists thing that sound is the most likely, since it could more accurately be measured by the bees, either by their antennae touching the dancer or by their feet picking up vibrations from the comb. Also, the sound is more accurately related to the distance (or rather, to the effort expended) than is the time of the run. While following the dancer, the bodies of the other bees do not point in the same direction as hers. Yet they can somehow perceive that direction and translate it into an angle from the sun. Not only that, but it has been shown that each bee has an internal clock which corrects for the movement of the sun across the sky. Thus she can change the angle of her flight as necessary, given the time of day.

9 · Other Bees and Wasps

Many other kinds of bees besides honeybees live in colonies. Some, such as bumblebees, have considerably smaller colonies with a simpler way of life, while other groups have colonies almost as large and complex as those of the honeybee. There are also many kinds of social wasps. How do these insects communicate with one another?

Finding Food

Do other kinds of bees also tell about food sources by dances? First let us look at the three closest relatives of the familiar type of honeybee. These are the Indian bee, the dwarf honeybee, and the giant honeybee. All three live in the tropics of India and southeast Asia. The Indian bee is very similar to our honeybee; it builds several combs in hollow trees and does round and waggle dances inside the dark hive. But this bee switches from a round dance to a waggle dance when the food source is only two yards from the hive.

The dwarf and the giant honeybee both have much smaller colonies than the common honeybee or the Indian bee. Each colony constructs a single comb which hangs down from a tree branch. The giant honeybee dances on the vertical surface of her comb, but the dancer must be able to see the sun while she dances or she gets confused. The dwarf honeybee, on the other hand, has a flat platform on top of the comb for dancing. In her dances, she points directly toward the food source. If the dance platform is covered so that there is no more horizontal surface for dancing, the bees become confused and cannot communicate with one another any more.

The stingless bees of South America have a well developed colony life, although it is simpler than that of the honeybee. Their "talk" about food sources is simpler, too. In many species, the successful forager merely runs about in the hive, bumping into other bees and making a high-pitched humming sound to alert new foragers. No distance or direction information is given.

But other stingless bees are just as thorough at communicating as are the honeybees. In these stingless species, the forager takes several trips alone to the food source. Then, on her way home, she stops frequently to deposit a pheromone from glands near her mouth on rocks and blades of grass. She returns to the hive and picks up a group of new bees which she leads along

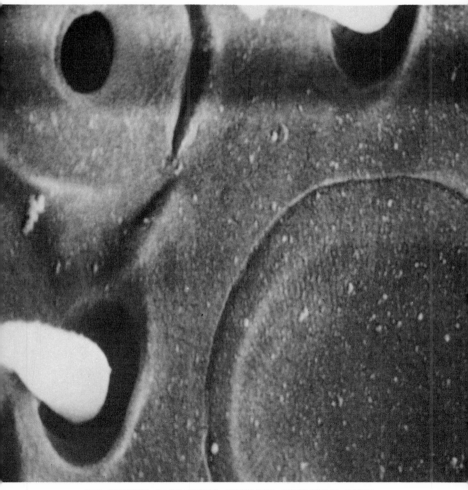

The antenna of a worker bee covered with minute white spines, seen at left and top, as well as holes, and circular plates called placodea—part of the system that senses odors. Photographed by a scanning electron microscope and reproduced at a magnification close to 15,000 times.

the odor trail to the food source. The smell of the odor trail is strong enough for even people to smell, but it seems the new recruits need both the odor trail and the guide bee the first time out to find the food.

In the dense tropical forest where the stingless bees live, an odor trail is a much better means of communication than a dance. The honeybee dance can communicate only the distance straight out from the hive. If honeybees are trained to a food source up high on a water tower, they are unable to communicate the location to their hive mates. Since honeybees live where flowers are reasonably close to the ground, they do not need a system which communicates up and down. But an odor trail can be deposited on leaves high above the ground as well as close to it. In the tropical forest, some blossoms are found high up, and an odor trail which can lead around dense foliage and up to a source of food is a definite advantage.

Molecules That Say "Danger!"

Alarm pheromones are found in a great variety of social bees and wasps. In species with small colonies, such as bumblebees and some wasps, an alarm substance is not necessary; any danger to the colony would be sensed by all the insects in the group at about the same time anyway. But when the colony is larger, a means of alerting all the members is necessary. Some wasps have an alarm substance in their venom. When one wasp is excited by danger, she turns her abdomen toward the threat and sprays venom. As well as being poisonous to intruders, the venom contains an alarm pheromone which smells like fermenting fruit. The molecules of this substance excite other wasps in the colony to turn and spray toward the enemy as well.

Some paper wasps have a different way of alerting the colony. The nests of these insects are fairly small and are attached by a thin stem. When an enemy such as a parasitic wasp is seen by a paper-wasp female near the nest, the paper-wasp first attacks the intruder, then flies around her nest, banging into the walls and causing the nest to vibrate. This alerts the other wasps, and they then dart about and flip their wings in excitement.

Robber Bees

Sometimes the same chemical is used by different species of social insects for different purposes. One particularly versatile substance is called citral. This is used as an alarm pheromone and defensive secretion by one ant while another uses it just for defense and responds to a different chemical with alarm. Citral is a strong attractant for honeybees, and is found in the secretion which they leave at a good food source. In one kind of stingless bee, citral is used as a trail-laying substance and apparently is also an alarm pheromone.

The most interesting use of citral is found in certain robber bees. These insects steal food from other kinds of bees rather than collect it on their own from flowers. It seems that the success of at least one kind of robber

bee depends on citral. When the robber bees attack a colony, the first scouts are likely to be killed by guard bees. But when they die, these scouts release the contents of enlarged glands near their mouths. These glands contain large quantities of citral. The citral fills the air around and inside the nest. More robber bees are attracted by the scent, while the citral inside the nest has a strange effect on the victim bees. Instead of defending their home, they wander about in a confused way, and many of the foragers and guards simply fly off and leave the nest defenseless. Thus the robbers can enter the nest and take whatever they want without a fight.

Scientists who have studied the behavior of robber bees have found that the three species of host bees normally attacked by the robbers all react to citral with

Several kinds of insects, including certain wasps and beetles, spray repellent chemicals at attackers. At top, an experimental setup shows a tethered Brachinus bombardier beetle about to be attacked by an ant. The middle picture shows the ant biting the beetle's leg, on which it gets a burst of hydroquinone solution that, through chemical action, heats it to boiling point. At the bottom, an Eleodes bombardier beetle goes into the characteristic headstand with which it responds to being disturbed; the next step will be to spray a quinonoid secretion at the attacker.

DR. THOMAS EISNER, DR. DANIEL ANESHANSLEY

confusion and abandoning the nest, while three other related species which the robbers do not attack are not affected by it in this way.

Compared to that of honeybees, the communication of other kinds of bees and wasps is little studied. However, scientists have found evidence of queen substances in some species and sex attractants in others. Bumblebee males, for example, mark out trails along established flying routes. These trails are thought to attract both male and female bumblebees so that mating can be assured. As more and more research is done in the field of wasp and bee communication, additional interesting examples which help our understanding of these remarkable animals will be found.

10 · Complicated Specialists:
The Termites

Termites are often called white ants. They live in colonies with workers, soldiers, and queens just as ants do. But termites are more closely related to cockroaches than to bees and ants.

If we study their colony life, we can see many important differences. Bees and ants are insects with true larvae, legless grubs which form pupae out of which emerge the adults. Termites hatch into six-legged, wingless "larvae" which molt many times as they grow and which may or may not become winged adults. These "larvae" are properly called nymphs. While worker bees and ants are females, termite workers and soldiers are both male and female. There is a king as well as a queen in the colony, or there may be several kings and queens.

We think of termites as pests which burrow into the

wooden parts of houses and eat them. But only a few kinds of termites actually live that way. Most termites live in tropical places and make their homes in the soil or build themselves "castles" above the ground, sometimes many feet tall. Termites are really quite fragile creatures and usually die if taken from their homes into the laboratory. Only a few species have been raised successfully by scientists, so little is known about the way of life of most termites.

All termites feed on wood and other materials containing the chemical substance cellulose. Most animals cannot digest cellulose, so termites have little or no competition for food. There are five families of "lower termites" which have special protozoa (one-celled creatures) living in their digestive tracts. These protozoa break down the cellulose into chemicals which the termites can digest. There is another family of "higher termites" which actually contain three-fourths of known living species. These animals have more complicated social organization than the lower termites and do not have protozoa to help digest the cellulose (it is not known for sure if these termites can digest cellulose themselves or if the bacteria which live in their digestive tracts do it). The familiar wood-dwelling termites are lower termites. Since the higher termites are very difficult to raise in the laboratory, scientific studies of termite communication have been done largely with a few lower species.

Caste Determination

The caste system of termites is much more complicated than that of bees and ants. Since adult bees and ants do not molt, the caste of an individual must be determined while it is a larva. With termites, however, a different situation exists. The animals molt many times and can stay at the same stage or change with each molt. In the one species of termite which has been studied in detail, the workers are actually individuals which can molt into soldiers, winged adults, or wingless reproductive forms. The queen and king produce pheromones which keep the workers from becoming reproductive types. If the king and queen die or are removed from the colony, some of the workers will molt into wingless replacement reproductives. If the soldiers are removed, some of the workers will molt into soldiers, so soldiers also probably produce inhibiting pheromones. In this way a proper balance of the different castes is kept up.

A very clever German scientist named Martin Luscher has done experiments which make clear the means of communicating the need for members of the different castes. In one interesting experiment, he divided a termite colony in half with a wire gauze fence. On one side of the fence was a group which had reproductive individuals, but there were none on the other side. The group without reproductives produced them

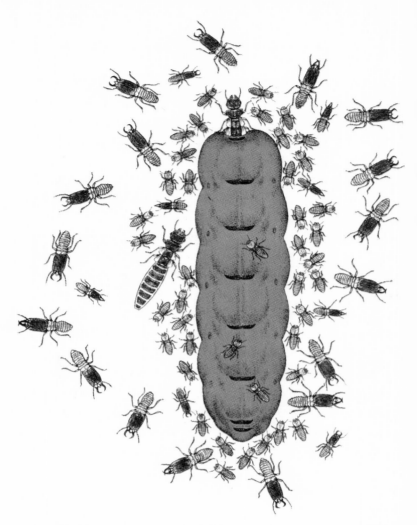

A termite queen tremendously swollen with eggs, surrounded by workers, a single king, and around the edge
in guard positions, the large-headed soldiers. The dark
bars on the queen's back are sclerites, described earlier.
Odors, sounds, and touch all help keep the elaborate
termite society working efficiently.

by the molting of some workers. But soon the workers in the group killed the new reproductives. If a double gauze fence was used, however, the reproductives were allowed to live. When only a single fence was present, the workers could put their antennae through the holes in the gauze and sense the contact pheromones of reproductives on the other side. With the double fence, they could not do so.

This experiment and others have shown that two completely different kinds of pheromones are involved in regulating the castes. The reproductive animals produce chemicals which are passed throughout the colony, by means of termites' feeding one another. These substances prevent the development of more reproductives. When the queens and kings die, the substance is no longer there, and some of the workers molt into reproductives. In the experiment, the single gauze prevented mutual feeding between the two halves of the colony, so the workers on the other side received none of these pheromones. Thus some molted into reproductives. But the remaining workers could still sense the surface pheromones of the kings and queens on the other side of the gauze. To them, their new reproductives were unneeded extras and were therefore killed.

Termite Alarm Bells

Sound, touch, and scent all seem to be involved in termite alarm systems. The soldiers of some higher termites use chemical alarms. They have large heads with very sharp, strong, curved jaws and are very aggressive. When disturbed, they squirt an alarm substance from their heads which causes them and other soldiers to snap and bite wildly. Other higher termites can squirt large quantities of strong chemicals from their heads,

DR. THOMAS EISNER

A group of soldier termites guarding a column of workers in a Panamanian rain forest. These soldiers are, in effect, ambulatory spray guns; through the long nozzle at the front of the head they spray at intruders a sticky, irritating fluid. Other types of soldiers, which rely mainly on fighting with their mandibles, or jaws, have oversize heads mostly filled with powerful muscles to operate them.

but in their case the chemicals serve more for defense than for alarm. Upon contact with the air, these substances become sticky and can trap small enemies such as ants so that they cannot move.

In many kinds of termites, disturbed individuals bang their heads or abdomens against the ground or roof. This causes vibrations which can be sensed by the others in the colony. Although many scientists think that alarm is communicated by these sounds, no one has actually proven so by experiments. In Chapter 1 the head-banging behavior of one species of termite is described. The scientist who studied this signal felt that it helped spread news of danger quickly to all members of the colony. This could be called a general alarm signal. Some scientists, however, feel that the head-banging is not an alarm signal but rather excites the workers, raising their level of activity when the nest is damaged. Excited by the thumps, workers would thus rebuild faster.

When there is a small injury to a termite nest, the alarm signal is more clear-cut. If a termite discovers a break, it runs toward the inside of the nest. As it runs, it drags its abdomen along the ground, leaving a pheromone trail. The alarmed animal runs in a zigzag path, bumping against other termites as it goes. These other individuals become alarmed and follow the pheromone trail to its start. When they reach the danger, they react to it by attack or rebuilding efforts. If the job is too big, they in turn run back into the nest, laying a trail

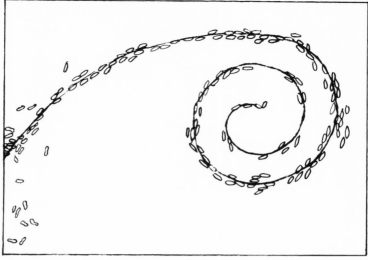

Pheromones have a strong effect on termites, as this experiment shows. A scent trail was drawn in a spiral with a very diluted solution of the insects' trail pheromone; as they came from their stock chamber at left they came upon the trail and are following it to the end, though a spiral trail is not one that occurs in their lives normally. Based on research by Dr. B. P. Moore.

and bumping into others along the way. When enough termites have joined the work force and the job is complete, no more trails are laid and the alarm dies out.

In higher termites, trail-laying also serves to guide workers to food. Unlike the familiar wood termites, these nest-building animals leave their homes to gather food. Pheromone trails allow the foragers to find their way between the nest and the food. It is interesting that in two such distantly related insects as termites and ants, the same system for successful foraging has evolved.

11 · Some Other Invertebrates

Since no other invertebrate land animals form complicated colonies consisting of many separate individuals such as those of the social insects, it is not surprising to find that most communication among these animals is related to mating. There are some exceptions, however. The females of some spiders cooperate in web-building, capture of prey, and even care of the brood, but study on their communication has barely begun. Repellent alarm pheromones are released in the slime of hurt earthworms. The males of some invertebrates act aggressively toward one another, which helps them to maintain territories. The territories usually are important in mating success.

Crab Signals

The communication systems of only a few crustaceans have been studied. There is evidence that sex pheromones produced by females attract the males in several different aquatic crustaceans. Communication by sight is important to many crustaceans, especially to the shore-dwelling fiddler crabs. Each male fiddler has his own burrow. One of his claws is greatly enlarged and is waved like a semaphore to attract the female and repel any males which come too close to his home. There are many species of fiddler crab, and each has its own mating display, and its own aggressive display.

One kind of fiddler crab has been especially well studied. In this species, the male raises his claws when he sees a female. He then extends them to the side and lowers them, at the same time lowering his body. If the female comes closer, he speeds up his routine, then backs up toward his burrow while still waving. If she follows, he enters the burrow, keeping his enlarged

A male fiddler crab, Uca minax, *waving its enlarged claw in part of the gesture that attracts females. The entire gesture takes two and a half seconds and is then repeated as long as necessary. Based on research by Dr. Michael Salmon.*

claw sticking out of the entrance. Then he thumps it rapidly against the ground to draw her nearer. If the female is ready to mate, she enters the burrow.

When another male comes along, the resident male turns so that the flattened, enlarged side of his claw is facing toward the intruder. If this doesn't scare him off, the two come together, the flat sides of their claws touching. They then push one another around until one gives up. If both are very stubborn, they may lock claws and try to flip one another over. When male animals fight each other over territories or females, they rarely are injured. The "fight" consists of a series of threatening moves which show which animal is stronger and more determined without drawing blood.

Male fiddler crabs recognize the sex of other crabs by the size of their claws. If the large claw of a male is removed, he is treated like a female by other males.

Scorpions' Courtship Language

Touch and vision are the main senses used in the communication of scorpions. When a male finds a female, he lifts his claws and jerks his body backward and forward very rapidly three or four times. Then he pauses and repeats this "juddering" movement. A responsive female simply lies quietly, watching him. He may move closer to her between bouts of juddering, and if she stays still, he will come forward and grab her claws in his. He pulls her close to him and grabs her mouth parts in his, then lets go of her claws. Now the two begin a peculiar dance, which probably serves, at least partly, to prepare them both for mating. The male walks backward and forward, pushing and pulling the female along with him. At first she may resist, but then she becomes passive. This stage may last for only a few minutes or for as long as an hour.

Then the male begins to scrape up the soil beneath his body, clearing away larger particles as he moves back and forth. After an area is clear, he deposits a

A whip scorpion shooting out its aimed spray on being experimentally pinched on its front leg. The whip scorpion is closely related to the true scorpions. DR. THOMAS EISNER

Spiders and other arachnids use their front legs as antennae. This wolf spider is raising its legs, which are covered with spines; the spines probably help in locating prey, and perhaps a mate, but this has not been proved as yet.

special structure called a spermatophore on the ground. This contains sperms. Now the female is jerked forward by the male until the opening of her reproductive tract is right over the spermatophore. Hooks on the spermatophore catch on her body next to the opening, and the sperms flow in while the two animals wait quietly. Then they separate.

Spiders' Mating

The elaborate courtship patterns of many species of spiders have been studied. They involve sight, scent, and sensing of vibrations in almost all spiders, and in some, sound may be involved also. The evolution of these complicated courtship displays has a very important effect: the males are protected from being eaten by the very aggressive females. The rituals of courtship allow the male to test the mood of the female from a safe distance before attempting to mate.

When a male of a web-building spider is ready to mate, he begins to wander. If he runs into the web of a female, he can recognize it as such by its odor. He then plucks at the threads with a special "Morse code" signal. If the female is not ready to mate, her reaction is aggressive, and the male leaves. If she is ready, she either is passive or signals back. He then enters the web and they mate.

The males of hunting spiders which lack a web find the female from the pheromone on the silk dragline which she produces as she wanders about. When he senses this female aroma, he begins his display. The males of these types of spiders have striking bands of white or colors on their legs which may help the female recognize males of her own kind. The males wave their legs and their palps, which are leglike appendages in front of the legs. They may also drum their palps on the ground. A responsive female will wave her forelegs in return, and move closer to the male. Her reaction increases the speed of his display.

The males of almost all spiders are willing to begin a courtship display at the merest excuse. An image in a mirror, another male of their own kind, or another kind of spider, may set him off. But the female can recognize the courtship display of her own kind and responds accordingly.

There are still other examples of communication systems we could explore—color changes in squid and octopus, pheromones in snails, and so forth. But the communication of most invertebrates other than insects and spiders is little known. Probably the future will bring new studies which will tell us more about this exciting field of knowledge.

Suggested Reading

Books

Philip Callahan, *Insect Behavior* (Four Winds, N.Y., 1970)

Olive Earle, *Crickets* (Morrow, N.Y., 1957)

Karl von Frisch, *The Dancing Bees* (Methuen and Co., London; Harcourt, Brace, N.Y., paperback, 1954)

————, *The Dance Language and Orientation of Bees* (Belknap Press of Harvard University Press, Cambridge, 1967)

D. C. Ipsen, *What Does a Bee See?* (Addison-Wesley, Reading, Mass., 1971)

Bernice Kohn, *Fireflies* (Prentice-Hall, Englewood Cliffs, N.J., 1966)

Peter Limburg, *Termites* (Hawthorn Books, N.Y., 1974)

Robert McClung, *Bees, Wasps, and Hornets* (Morrow, N.Y., 1971)

Ernestine J. Norsgaard, *Insect Communities* (Grosset and Dunlap, N.Y., 1973)

Lynn D. Poole and Gray J. Poole, *Fireflies in Nature and the Laboratory* (Crowell, N.Y., 1965)

Hilda Simon, *Exploring the World of Social Insects* (Vanguard, N.Y., 1962)

Magazine Articles

Richard D. Alexander, "The Evolution of Cricket Chirps," *Natural History*, Nov. 1966

H. C. Bennet-Clark and A. W. Ewing, "The Love Song of the Fruitfly," *Scientific American*, July 1970

Martin Birch, "Persuasive Scents in Moth Sex Life," *Natural History*, Nov. 1967

Lee Ehrman and Monroe W. Strickberger, "Flies Mating: a Pictorial Record," *Natural History*, Nov. 1960

Harold Esch, "The Evolution of Bee Language," *Scientific American*, April 1967

Karl von Frisch, "Dialects in the Language of the Bees," *Scientific American*, Aug. 1962

R. Gannon, "Fireflies: Nature's Light Fantastic," *Frontiers*, June 1967

Bert Hölldobler, "Communication Between Ants and Their Guests," *Scientific American*, March 1971

Martin Jacobson and Morton Beroza, "Insect Attractants," *Scientific American*, Aug. 1964

Jack Colvard Jones, "The Sexual Life of a Mosquito," *Scientific American*, April 1968

John C. Moser, "Trails of the Leafcutters," *Natural History*, Jan. 1967

Marc Roth, L. M. Roth, and T. E. Eisner, "The Allure of the Female Mosquito," *Natural History*, Dec. 1966

Theodore Savory, "Courtship Behavior of Arachnids," *Natural History*, May 1965

William G. Wellington, "A Special Light to Steer By," *Natural History*, Dec. 1974 (polarized light)

Adrian M. Wenner, "Sound Communication in Honeybees," *Scientific American*, April 1964

Edward O. Wilson, "Pheromones," *Scientific American*, May 1963

———, "Animal Communication," *Scientific American*, Sept. 1972

Paul A. Zahl, "Wing-borne Lamps of the Summer Night," *National Geographic*, July 1962

———, "Nature's Night Lights: Probing the Secrets of Bioluminescence," *National Geographic*, July 1971

Index